Off Road

Off Road

Four wheel drive vehicles in colour

Andrew Morland

OSPREY

Published in 1982 by Osprey Publishing Limited
12-14 Long Acre, London WC2E 9LP
Member company of the George Philip Group

British Library Cataloguing in Publication Data
Morland, Andrew
Off road: four wheel drive vehicles in colour.
—(Automotive colour paperback)
1. Automobiles—Four wheel drive—Pictorial works
I. Title   II. Series
629.2'2'0222   TL230.5.F6

ISBN 0-85045-446-8

Editor Tim Parker

Printed in Hong Kong

Any motor manufacturer produces what he thinks he can sell. Utility vehicles with four wheel drive, all terrain capability are an acknowledged market sector with a number of such companies agreeing substantially to its profile without constant consultation. Land Rover in Britain and Jeep in the United States are the best known for their rivalry in this game. Both started just postwar and had the next decade more or less to themselves. No one rode in one of their excellent products unless he had to!

Along came the 1960s and for some reason the Americans started to turn the purely utilitarian workhorse into something to have fun in. At the same time, and certainly not just because of that, other manufacturers started producing deadly rivals—Toyota in Japan, for example. Bingo! By the 1970s there were two markets—the old, still substantial utlitarian but also the new recreational, which might just be larger. More manufacturers turned their hand worldwide.

By the 1980s everyone is affected by the macho, aggressive, huge, high off-road vehicle.

This all colour book brings out the magic of the off road four wheel drive, go anywhere vehicle in both utilitarian and recreational guises but without shame it majors on the latter. Search within its pages for dune buggies, mud pluggers, swamps buggies, racing rails, Jeeps, Land Rovers, 4WD pick-ups, Broncos, Ramchargers, Baja Bugs and many more familiar names in the international off road scene.

Shielded from the sun, his head by a cotton hat and his lens by its hood, professional photographer Andrew Morland enjoys himself on the desert near Ocotillo, on the Mexican border in California.

Both Andrew and the editor had a lot of help when trying to create this book. In alphabetical order we are grateful to the following: All Wheel Drive Club (GB); Anonymous couple who pulled a CJ7 Jeep and a Range Rover off the shingle at the Chesil Beach with a smoky 20 year old Land Rover and 100 foot rope—we were stuck; Gleeson Civil Engineering Ltd, North Cheam, Surrey; Tony Hogg, editor of *Road & Track* magazine; Jeep (UK) Ltd; Lada Cars (GB) Ltd; Land Rover Ltd; Rich McCormack of The Newport Press, California; Mercedes-Benz (United Kingdom) Ltd; Nissan Motor Co—USA (Datsun); Mike Pearce; Philippine Airlines; Subaru (UK) Ltd; Beth and Charlie Tutt (Pikes Peak).

Contents

Jeep—twice as much drive?

Left Although on Virginian plates this stock CJ7 Renegade Jeep is at Old Tucson, Arizona. V8 power makes it one of America's most costly to insure. **Below** 'Beach Boys'—Pismo Beach in CA is one of the last dune areas which can still be used, or abused, by off-roaders however laid-back. Note smiles

Above CJ6 at Azusa Canyon, California. The dried up river bed provides an ideal play park for such vehicles. Goodyear Wrangler R/T tyres compliment wide after-market 'mags'. **Right** Swamp buggy racing—wheels mostly on the deck—gets popular. Here, at Naples in the Everglades in South Florida, various Jeeps seem to work

Waterproofing is obviously essential for this game. No mean task. Each driver/passenger seem to have different ideas as to how deep the swamp is. Naples, Florida

Left No conventional four wheel driver can hope to handle shingle like this. There was no traction whatsoever. This new CJ7 Renegade with the 'economy' but still lusty 4 cylinder needed a winch. Chesil Beach, Dorset. **Above** In right hand drive form this 1981 CJ7 (93½ inch wheelbase) was an endearing vehicle. With arm waving it could stay with a Range Rover on tarmac. Not off road, though. Wiltshire grain drying silos provide backdrop

Front nerf bar is an English accessory. 'Sloane Ranger' Renegade climbed Shaftesbury's famous Gold Hill (*Far from the Madding Crowd*) without bother

Izusu diesel or Toyota petrol engines power the majority of Jeepneys. Both 2 and 4 wheel drive is seen. Speed is no problem with the petrol engine. The Jeepney bus can be hailed like a taxi. Monsoon time here

Bus park in the Philippines. Manilla streets, and elsewhere, are crowded with some 27,000 Jeepneys. First built by Mr Clod Delfino from an American Army leftover Willys; today they are custom built

Above Mobile shoe shop via Ebis. Selling flip flops. Perhaps the stack on the bonnet front help to compensate for the enormous rear overhang **Right** British Jeep racer appropriately called Black Power. This Willys has Daimler power with its 2½ litre push-rod V8. The jump is on the tank range at Aldershot, home of the British army. Rare UK registered Land Cruiser in the background

Land Rover – reputation across the world

Off road enthusiasts had long been fitting the Range Rover V8 in the simpler Land Rover. Here's a superb example of the factory's long overdue V8 Station Wagon on Brean Sands in Somerset. 'Built and designed to go anywhere'

Above Marshalls' vehicles at an AWDC meeting at Bovington, Dorset. Left is a lightweight, ex army 88 inch wheelbase of indeterminate age in a livery of the type made popular by Simmonites of Bradford; right is a 1972 Hardtop Land Rover. **Right** Series I Land Rover at speed at Aldershot. Vehicles of this 1950's vintage are cheap to buy and easy to race. This one is Dave Buckingham's rear-mid engined version; its standard axles are turned upsidedown!

Above Typical of the superb engineering which can be seen in the UK for a racing special. Essentially this is a Range Rover. Even with mild tuning the engine can produce 200 hp. Practice run only, no helmet, for 1981 AWDC Gatton Manor champion Nick Johns. **Right** Fighting for grip. Even the special front suspension of this Land Rover can be defeated in dry sand like this. This one would not be street legal

Left Racing at Bordon is fun but filthy. This heavily cutaway (a standard
88 inch Land Rover weighs around 3000 lb) racer looks like an ex army
conventionally bodied version. **Above** Very stock except for the roll cage just
visible. The tank track network at Bovington provides regular off road racing.
This Series I Land Rover isn't going to win, but there's no denying the fun

This 1964 swb 'cab and open rear body' needed man power to unstick itself here at Aldershot. External roll cage is a popular British modification

Although only of 1977 vint
this Land Rover was the m
abused seen during this
assignment. Still going str
with no servicing but alwa
off road on construction si
Never cleaned either

Brean Sands in Somerset engulf at least one vehicle
per year. The 109 inch V8 Station Wagon comes
built-in with many new features, plus exciting
colours like this red

Right top The Range Rover 4 door with 'custom pack', something new for the factory. Apart from cast alloy wheels, clearly visible, this superb vehicle had two LPG tanks. Gentleman image should not belittle vehicle's capability. **Above** No one can deny the luxury of this Range Rover. Both on and off the road this 4 door is a pleasure to drive and ride in. **Right bottom** Outside Camelware House, Somerset. New 4 door Range Rover comes with low compression, aluminium 3528 cc V8. LPG option, although doubling the vehicle's range, makes it slower still. Tarmac cruising is still close to 90 mph

Above This is the Range Rider, a special lightweight cutdown Range Rover, the second racing vehicle built by doyen of the British off road scene Alvin Smith. Driven here by its new owner at Weaver's Down, Bordon it was first fitted with an Australian built 4.4 litre 'Rover' alloy engine. It was fast. Sponsors Schuler market automatic and 5 speed transmissions for Range Rovers. **Right top** This ex military lightweight 88 inch Land Rover has been beautifully prepared for off road racing. Its engine is unknown but is unlikely to be any of LR's own. Popular transplants are now the ex Oldsmobile Rover V8. **Right bottom** Bordon racing in 1977. This Series IIA pick-up features Range Rover wheels (the trick set-up) and some Jeep influence with the screen. This shot shows the ideal racing terrain

Left Strange Rover—Triumph TR7 bodyshell on Alvin Smith Range Rover mechanicals. New owner Keith Gott finds the vehicle fast but claustrophobic and its difficult to see the terrain ahead because of the front overhang. In Alvin's day it was also a rally car actually finishing the Welsh International in 1980. **Above** One of the best of a number of modified Range Rovers. Called the Unitruck, it is designed to suit the agrochemical industry. 4 seats, LPG power, sealed cab and more. Idea—Mike Pearce and David Chaffey; construction—Corville Auto Engineers, Sherborne, Dorset

VW–2WD but universal

Below Beetle made in Southern California! Commonly known as a Baja Bug this bright projectile hasn't been radically altered, in fact. Most of it bolts on. This beauty will go best on the Coast Highway on which it sits, not the desert.

Left A second Baja Bug but using another company's kit. Note the roof oil cooler (back) and driving lights (front). Rear screen is punched out. Azusa Canyon watering hole, California's interior

Above VW flat four power in this Pikes Peak hillclimber.
Canadian Bill Warner spits dust in his 1975 Newman Dreager VW
sponsored by Sunshine Rentals. Built for the job. **Right** Delightful
Pikes Peak shot. Approaching the Devil's Playground on the way
up is Danny Arant in his home-built Grizzly VW. Obvious is the
different thinking in chassis design as to the perfect dirt-surface
hillclimber

Left So hot, the canal looks like tarmac. Here at Glamis, near Mexicali, an umbrella helps only a little. Paddle sand rear tyres dominate this VW-powered rail. The event here was cancelled; it was too hot **Above** Home produced, but one of many, this VW sand rail uses a VW 1600 'upright fan' motor. Husband and wife team run in the desert near Ocotillo, close to the Mexican border in California. It's very hot

Light weight and good traction avoid
the need for four wheel drive in this
desert terrain. The ubiquitous VW
supplies most of the parts for this rail.
The steering comes from a Ford
Pinto—few like the VW 'box'

Above The VW 181 Thing built in Mexico but seen here in Encinatas, California. Conceived when the off road scene was growing as a sort of modern *Kubelwagen*. This one has non-stock wheels. Off road capability, nil **Right** Anything goes. This split-screen Microbus has the familiar hugh cutouts for oversize rear tyres. Because it's essentially Beetle a lot of suitable equipment is available to increase its off road capability. Azusa Canyon again

On the streets in America's West

Front plates are not obligatory in California. Front grille and
headlamps suggests that this is a 1978 Ford Custom (more
comfortable Ford Ranger with Mohave embossed vinyl seat trim!).
Actually another F-100 Regular Cab with Styleside bed

rican Motors know a lot
t four wheel drive. This
a Eagle 2 door 4WD, in
words a much modified
C Concord Deluxe with
influenced running gear.
irsty but effective, fun
. Chino, near Riverside,
California

Another Ford Ranger pic[
of '78/79 vintage in the Y[
Desert. The Ford F ser[
brochure says 'Ford Tru[
are famous for their [
toughness'. Engine opti[
range from 300 six to 46[

The familiar *adobe hacienda* confirm the location.
Actually Santa Fe. Two door Jeep Cherokee Chief
(5900 cc V8, 3 speed auto QuadraTrac, and a curb
weight of 3858 lb). Shop's called Suzette, the
motorcycle's a Harley

Right Ford's Jeep equivalent comes not from their often 2 wheel drive F series but as the Bronco. This XLT custom pack treatment is pretty common now. Little off road work for this one, though **Above** Yet another standard, factory supplied paint scheme on a Ford Bronco, shot in Manitou Springs, Colorado. Black paint can't be good for the temperature inside the vehicle. Air conditioning usually sorts it out

Keen off-road new car sales lot. This man sells Ford and Jeep at Dana Point, on the Coast Highway in California. Ford F-150 Ranger has Regular Cab, a Styleside bed of 6¾ feet

brewing over Colorado
rings. Chrysler/Dodge
dealer has pinstriped
charger with whitewall
, nerf bar and roll bar-
ted driving lamps—no
off road tyres yet

Above Further down the lot is this handsome factory-painted blue and white Dodge Power Ram. V8 power is fun but is getting too expensive to run. These large pick-ups are now losing sales to the mini pick-ups **Right** Chevy Stepside pick-up resting at Brunt's Corner Dr Pepper at Gila Bend, noted truckstop. Stepside bed is throwback to the pronounced rear 'mudguard' look of the late 1930s

Just a fun truck although
without four wheel drive.
very stock Chevrolet 'big'
pick-up on the Arizona
highway in the Apache
Mountains **Right** Ford's
F Series 'Freewheeling
Flareside' (their stepside) with
in style customizing. One-
off mural, stacks, cab step,
trim, roll bar, wheel arch
flares, wheels and finally
paint

Above Passenger enjoyed his burger. Typical everyday highway scene (on the way to Albuquerque). Well used Ford F series 4WD pick-up is specially raised on its suspension for soft off roading **Right** The Ford F series is very popular. Here's a near new F-250 Regular Cab but with 8 foot Styleside Cargo box. Datsun is 1981 King Cab 4WD. Azusa Canyon, CA

Off highway – mega fun

Left Not yet downsized this recent 'full size' Chevy near Oceanside, CA, still runs a 305 inch V8. Wheels are special, the rest is stock. Unlike the Jeep's door mirrors, you look at them through the door window. **Below** 4D BIRDS. Big Cherokee Chief 2 door and small tent on the sand at Pismo Beach. Note feet behind the windscreen. Better than taking that monster into the dunes

Above Nelly's Ford Bronco with the faithful 302 inch V8 aboard. This must be an early Bronco (first introduced in 1965). The snow confirms its Pikes Peak, Colorado **Right** Spectator park at Pikes Peak, Colorado. This F series Ford pick-up shows off American life—cowboy hat, beer can and 'chocolate chip cookie' bag!

Top Off road but too low for four wheel drive. This ex public service Chevy Custom 10 Stepside has hidden teeth, a transplanted 7 litre V8 for 300 hp. Dog's are more frightening, lady's just pearls. **Above** Is the boulder there for the lack of a handbrake (unnecessary with auto transmission) or has it just been climbed by this Chevrolet Cheyanne Stepside. Ford Ranger just behind. Pikes Peak, Colorado. **Right** Jacked-up and mildly customized. This short F-100 ($6\frac{1}{2}$ foot Cargo box with 117 inch wheelbase) Ford is built just for fun. Here, at Azusa Canyon. Paint is more elaborate than factory's Tu-Tone

Chevy Van custom-converted to four wheel drive. Big
winch protudes in front of the grille but behind the
nerf bar. Anyone stuck knows the strength of a good
winch

'. . . fun, fun, fun till daddy takes the winch *away'*.
Azusa Canyon is the perfect playground for off
roaders. Don't think the Ford pick-up is stuck

ft Water and mud must
y hell with diff seals and
kes, let alone the clutch.
 with winch about to haul
 evy without. Breaking
n of the cable must be at
st 5000 lb. Heavy work.
Right It appears that
usiasts have dug this hole
pecially to get stuck in.
e again the winch ensures
ne ever lose their trucks
 together. Twist on that
pick-up is frightening

Channel 17 advertising with CB handle; Mud Plugger
helps anyone with his International Scout. Rough,
tough but ugly off road vehicle

pectacular shot. This is
in Utah. Pick-up appears
be a Chevy with a short
per on board. Touring
merica this way is most
satisfying

American antiques

Below Antique wrecker in Cripple Creek. It's still being used. It's a four wheel drive 1939 Ford 'I tonner' with 85 horsepower and hydraulic brakes (the first year). This one comes with a plate stating 'Marmon-Herrington All Wheel Drive'. Rust is not so damaging in America's south west. **Right** Dodge L6 four wheel drive truck of 1958, the first year with the quad headlamps. Part of the top grille is missing. Dodge had special tough vehicle status left over from the Second World War. Tucson, Arizona

Down Pikes Peak after it's all over for the spectators. First vehicle is a 1949 Chevy Styleline, a light panel truck cum Sedan Delivery equipped with 4WD. Second is 1957 Chevrolet Nomad. Third a Jeep

Left Conversions of this sort are common. The engineering has to be sound. So many components are currently available to do this that little will need to be custom made. Late '40s panel truck bodyshell is cute. **Top** Chevy's neat $\frac{1}{2}$ ton truck of 1955/56. V8 powered and their first model with 12 volt electrics. This one is neatly unrestored. As-new condition is common for area. Next door is a camper factory; Tucson, Arizona. **Above** Obviously not yet finished— some critics might even say that the 4WD conversion to this '57 Chevy Nomad (2 door estate) should never have begun. Door must have come from another model—trim doesn't match

The flat windscreen Chevy-Van of 1964. Came as standard with either a 90 hp four or 120 hp six, plus 2WD. This understated red van comes out of the Azusa mud hole with V8 and 4WD transplant

Above Burt Reynolds lookalike power washes his Ford Bronco (late '60s production) after Sunday's fun. Many have come to realise that stock appearance often hides trick set-ups—this is a good case in point **Right** 1968 Chevy El Camino ('caratruck') sits on Blazer running gear. Owner Steve Goeglein spent many hours pefecting this one. Pikes Peak landscape is spectacular

International Scout from International Harvester
better known for agricultural equipment, perhaps.
This one is modified and difficult to date accurately.
California

Japan's versatility—catching fast

Toyota feast. Resting at Azusa Canyon enjoying the
sun. Left to right: Land Crsuiser FJ40, a diesel engine
would have made it a BJ40; Hilux 4 × 4 mini
pick-up, well modified; Hilux 4 × 4, new and stock

Still a leader in small four wheel
drivers, Fuji Heavy Industries decided
America needed a pick-up. Hence the
Brat. Bed mounted seats use the cab
as a back rest. Appreciating the low
underbody clearance, Subaru's score.
Azusa Canyon lake

Right Subaru 1600 4WD 4 door saloon. On or off the road, towing a trailer or overloaded, this right hand drive version was superb. It did get stuck but only where a 4WD mini pick-up would have too. 1800 engine must be better still. Dartmoor, Devon. **Above** Suzuki's 'whizzer' 797 cc four cylinder, four wheel drive LJ80 nicknamed Saucy Suzy. This diminutive pick-up is race-prepared ready to start at Bovington, Dorset, England. A vast improvement from its predecessor, the Jimmy

Above Stock Suzuki. Smaller than the Daihatsu, it is easy to confuse one with the other from the back and sides. The fronts are more distinctive. Suzuki comes only with a petrol engine. **Left** Sun, shadow and dust. Stock Toyota Hilux 4 × 4 fooling around

Above Santa Ana Mountains, California. Datsun's latest King Cab now runs 98 hp from its overhead camshaft 4 cylinder 2.2 litre. 4WD equipment has become sophisticated. No one could mistake this for the 2WD version from behind. **Right top** Overlooking a lakeside village in the Santa Ana Mountains. This shot shows off the 'king cab' bit and factory paint job. Underbody clearance is 8.9 inches. **Right bottom** Unused road still provides suitable off roading in the Santa Ana Mountains. Datsun looks stable on thin but knobbly Bridgestone Desert Duellers

Above Toyota Land Cruiser was first produced in 1958. It's still in production in 1982 but with a brand new revised model. This one is impossible to date from this shot. For some they are the world's finest.

Left Early 1970's Toy Cruiser on the freeway, Mountain Springs Pass, up from San Diego. Most American versions are petrol engined. Now the factory are concentrating on the energy saving diesels

Europe's best – both sides of the Iron Curtain

Below The Russian-built Uaz (for Ulianvskij Automobilnij Zavod) comes to the UK as a Trekmaster. Available only as a forward-control with a 78 horsepower four cylinder 2466 cc petrol engine, it is very basic. With 2 or 4 wheel drive available, it's a cheap off road alternative. **Right** This is the 280GE Mercedes-Benz long wheel base estate in right hand drive form; it has the optional manual transmission. Developed with Steyr-Puch of Austria this has no mean cross-country ability. Two feet of wet chalk-mud couldn't stick it

Top Trunk road construction work by Gleeson Civil Engineering (A3/A30 link road in Hampshire) provides the back drop. Although the 280GE couldn't match the style of those dump trucks rushing to get through millions of tons of chalk, it could go where they went. **Above** Speed to avoid sticking was necessary even for the Mercedes in spite of low ratio four wheel drive and both axles difflocked (from inside the cab). Quality is impeccable, effectiveness superb although vehicle length can check motion sometimes. Tarmac speed for fuel injected six is high. **Right** Gleesons have dug and graded the new trunk road this far. The 280GE could climb the slope. Tinted windows show here. The Land Rover is there for scale. Short wheel base M-B even with diesel option matches the off road performance of this one

Above Lada Niva—everyone loved it in this custom
guise—here on Dartmoor. Off road ability was good,
on road fine, but noisy, with gears and tyres not
helping. Similar to a swb Land Rover the wheelbase is
88 inches. **Right** Lada engine is Fiat based 1570 cc
(with diesel option). Assembled in Russia on the banks
of the River Volga it has proven to be a tough,
competent off roader. Racing successes have come its
way too

Above Right hand drive Lada Niva (Vaz 2121 in some countries—Lada means a barn door in Swedish) is a UK conversion. Going off road needs two vehicles, one to tow out the other. A winch would be better too. Subaru 4WD saloon could cope with Dartmoor terrain, however. **Right** The UK imported Cournil is made in Portugal under licence from its French source. This racing version has a tuned Renault petrol engine although the regular version comes with a Peugeot diesel. Construction quality is high, so is the price

France is a nation of fanatical off roaders, their local custom builders run into hundreds No one seems to worry about exterior style, the Cournil is ugly but one of the most effective four wheel drive vehicles in the world. 100 inch wheelbase canvas, pick-up or hardtop

Close up

Below American bumper sticker. Such is the after-market accessory industry no two ever seem to be the same. **Bottom** Familiar Land Rover logo in its usual cast plate form. V8 part is just a decal, however. Tail lamps are mounted on aluminium plate rivetted to the alloy door. Land Rovers are still made at Solihull

Understated Subaru 4WD badge, bonnet mounted.
Note headlamp washers—wipers could be a better
fitment. The car is stuck, with one rear wheel in the
air, on Dartmoor

Pikes Peak is serious. This is a twin-turbo Porsche 911
engine expensively installed in the back of a hillclimb
chassis. A lot of care has been taken

Four shocks per side, per
axle, are the trick set-up.
Nestling behind this
immaculate rig is a set of
white Sperexed tubular headers
and some chromed suspension.
This is a mega-buck Chevy

More typical installation is this VW boxer engine.
Exhaust building is a highly skilled art

Arizona plate has been
modified to clear the Baja Bug
carburettor air filter.
Installation could have been
neater, driver's sentiment is
clear, however

Such has been the growth of off road motoring over the past 20 years, the California State now licences every off road vehicle. Neat plate here

Wheels and tyres for off roaders are so large that most spares have to be hung in sunlight. Shade covers proliferated. This Jeep tells you who the owners are rather than where they bought their truck

Two-wheel-drive

Left top Off road fun can come with two wheel drive and cheaply. Honda saw the market for a small, four wheeled motocross machine. The Odyssey comes with everything you need for such madness including high flotation rear tyres.
Left bottom Honda's 248 cc motocross (not yet water cooled for the Odyssey) has plenty of horsepower for everyday Azusa Canyon. Note Odyssey tyre tread in the slope in the background. **Below** If you have the strength, and courage, there is nowhere you can't go. Hot rod versions are around. Help!

1981 spec Odyssey comes in red instead of yellow
(usually), full roll cage, headlamp, and improved
suspension. Honda says 'As far as you can get from
sensible transportation. . . .' Three-wheeler in the
background is Honda's ATC

The French tend to power their off road racing chassis on Renault engines, usually ~~~ine tuned. Like the VW ~~~tle based chassis, Renault ~~xles are similarly used

Above Ralmondi buggy from France also uses an Alpine Renault engine and transaxle. Centrally mounted spark plugs give this away. This one seems to be running over-rich. **Right** Purpose built off road racing buggies are relatively rare in the UK. This one has come from America. Conditions are superb at Bordon

Left The French Punch buggy is an established race winner with a variety of engines fitted. This particular one uses a Citroën-Maserati engine, a 3 litre four cam V6, similar to those fitted in Citroën's SM and Maserati's Merak **Above** Ugly VW based buggy of the conventional sort. Speed at Bordon, Surrey comes from Ron Lamb's 1.7 litre boxer motor

Above One event per year for this $50,000 engined off road chassis. Built in 1979 this is just a twin-turbo Porsche Special belonging to Bruce Canepa Racing. His other car has but one turbo. Pikes Peak. **Right** Two wheel drive only but lots of horse-power of the right sort in the right chassis. Pikes Peak is difficult to win

Left Real swamp buggy in the Everglades, Florida. Is it a boat? **Above** With all the style in the world Matra have never made the Rancho four wheel drive. As it is, it's a good 'holdall' but with little cross country application. Its front wheel drive Talbot Alpine base could be modified. Sand yacht racing sponsorship at Brean Sands